What I Like

Where I Live

Liz Lennon

W

FRANKLIN WATTS

LONDON•SYDNEY

I love where I live.

My home, my family
and my town
are all here!

The postman knows where I live from my address.

My address says my house, my street, my town and my postcode.

I live in a block of flats in the city.

Look, I can see all the way
to the park from here.

I live in a village.
My best friend
lives nearby.

I play in my friend's garden.

On my street there are flats, houses and shops.

We buy our milk and bread
from the corner shop.

There is a shopping centre nearby.

It is full of shops.

The sweet shop is my favourite. **Yum!**

Every week we go on the
bus to the supermarket.

On the way, we
go past the library.
It is full of books!

I learned to swim at the swimming pool.

There's a slide there.

Wheee!

The park is my favourite place.

There is a playground there.

I like to go higher and higher on the swings!

Lots of people
work in this area.

My dad works in an office and my mum works at the hospital.

Sometimes we take the train to visit my aunt in the country.

But I like my area best – it's where I live!

About this book

The locality a child lives in is central to their world. This includes their home, street and all the local public places. Talking about all these things will help children realise they are a part of a local community and that there are lots of these around the world. Looking at and talking about the pictures is a good starting point. Here are some ideas for further talking points:

Address Do they know their address? What street do they live on? What is it like? What do they like best about their area?

Homes What is their home like? Is it a flat, house or something else? What do they have in it? What do they like about it?

Local places Are there shops local to them? Which is their favourite? What else? Perhaps there is a library or swimming pool. What other local public places can they think of?

People at work What kind of workplaces are there in their local area? Think about farming, factories, offices, schools etc. Who are the people who help them in the local area? Think about teachers, librarians, the police, the fire service and health services.

Outside their area What other places have they travelled to? Have they been to another town for sight-seeing, to visit family or to go shopping? What was similar about the other town? What was different?

First published in 2011
by Franklin Watts

Copyright © Franklin Watts 2011

Franklin Watts
338 Euston Road
London NW1 3BH

Franklin Watts Australia
Level 17/207 Kent Street
Sydney, NSW 2000

All rights reserved.

Dewey number: 643.1
ISBN: 978 1 4451 0468 3

Printed in China

Series Editor: Sarah Peutrill
Art Director: Jonathan Hair
Series Designer: Paul Cherrill
Picture Researcher: Diana Morris
Consultants: Karina Philip
and Deborah Cox

Franklin Watts is a division of
Hachette Children's Books,
an Hachette UK company.
www.hachette.co.uk

Every attempt has been made to
clear copyright. Should there be any
inadvertent omission please apply to
the publisher for rectification.

Picture credits:
Alamy: Christina Kennedy 5;
Photofusion PL 11; Alex Segre 10.
Corbis: Jon Feingersh Photography
21; Ocean 14. Franklin Watts: Chris
Fairclough 22t. istockphoto: Justin
Horrocks 8; René Mansi 20; Henrique
NDR Martins 15; Daniel Rodriguez 23;
Marzanna Syncerz 1, 9. Shutterstock:
Aljabak 6; Benis Arapovic 18; Evgenly
Ayupov front cover, 19; Stephen
Coburn 4; gemphotography 13; Morgan
Lane Photography 3; Pavel Losevsky
16, 17; Petr Malyshev 22b; OPIS 7;
Prism68 12; sming 2.